I See Insects

Stink Bug

written by **August Hoeft**

xist Publishing

INSPIRING DISCOVERY & DELIGHT

I see a stink bug.

The stink bug is brown and green.

The stink bug has
long antennae.

7

The stink bug
eats leaves.

The stink bug lives on plants.

11

I see a stink bug.